*Presented to*

Heather Pearson

*On* Oct. 9, 2022

*By*

# A Word to My Sponsor

Celebrating the Life
of Your Godchild

Richard and Hazel Bimler

CONCORDIA PUBLISHING HOUSE · SAINT LOUIS

*This booklet is dedicated to our sponsors
and godchildren:*

*Bill, Caroline, Ed, Ann,
Cheryl, Kim, Tom, Mark,
Jimmie, Lisa, and Jill.*

*Thanks for sharing the baptismal promise
with us!*

This edition published 2013 by Concordia Publishing House
3558 S. Jefferson Avenue
St. Louis, MO 63118-3968
1-800-325-3040 • www.cph.org

Text © 1998 Concordia Publishing House

Scripture quotations from the ESV Bible® (The Holy Bible, English Standard Version®), copyright © 2001 by Crossway Bibles, a publishing ministry of Good News Publishers. Used by permission. All rights reserved.

Sections of the Rite of Holy Baptism taken from *Lutheran Service Book*, copyright © 2006 Concordia Publishing House. All rights reserved.

Manufactured in the United States of America

12  13  14  15  16  17  18      20  19  18  17  16  15

# Contents

# Your Godchild's Special Day

Name _____

Date _____

Congregation _____

Address _____

    Scripture Lessons _____

    _____

    Parent(s) _____

    _____

    Sponsor(s) _____

    _____

    Other Special People Who Attended

    _____

    _____

    _____

    _____

    Pastor _____

    Special Stories or Observations of the Day

    _____

    _____

    _____

# Introduction

A splash of water.

The words of promise: "In the name of the Father and of the Son and of the Holy Spirit . . ."

A community of believers . . .

Another Baptism as the Lord marks a person as His forgiven child!

And because of this action by our Lord, we continue to live out our daily Baptism each day as members of the family of God.

This booklet focuses on the power and promise of God first shared with each of us at our own Baptism. It is intended for baptismal sponsors of infants, children, youth, and even adults. The following pages remind each of us of God's daily promise to us through our Baptism and encourage us to live out this promise with those around us, especially with those who call us sponsors. The book also emphasizes the fact that our Lord continues to be the "sponsor" for each of us as He calls, gathers, enlightens, and makes us holy each and every day.

These pages will provide some practical ideas, prayers, questions, and activities designed to help you live out your baptismal promise with those around you. The activities also are intended to focus on the joys and celebration of Baptism as they serve as daily reminders of the promise God has given to each of us in our Savior, Jesus Christ.

Baptism is God's gift of love, affirmation, and belonging. It is God "calling us by name" (Isaiah 43:1) and making us His own. And no one will ever take away that promise! Not even when we forget whose we are or when we forget to remember those who call us sponsor.

We are renewed and refreshed in knowing that God continues to hug us for the sake of Jesus through the power of Baptism.

Baptism is a daily event. Five-year-old Rachel expressed this well. She and Grandpa had been discussing Baptism informally for several weeks when one day she spilled lemonade all over the kitchen table. Grandpa became a little upset, especially because Grandma wasn't around to help clean up the mess. As Grandpa began helping Rachel clean up the sticky stuff, Rachel, sensing Grandpa's irritation, looked at him and exclaimed, "Well, I still am baptized, aren't I?"

Enough said. Case closed. Baptism is a daily occurrence. It is a constant reminder of God's promise through Jesus that has been given to each of us—to Rachel and even to Grandpa—to love, accept, and forgive, even in sticky situations.

# How Do You Spell Baptism?

Use these thoughts to instigate making Baptism a daily event in your life, as well as in the life of your godchild.

**B** stands for *BE*. Baptism tells us who we are. We are human beings, loved and redeemed by Christ. Our Baptism seals this promise of redemption in our lives. Being one of God's people, forgiven in Christ, assures us of life eternal and helps us to live each day as a gift from the Lord.

**A** stands for *AFFIRM*. Baptism affirms us! It says we are special people. It marks us with the sign of the cross, through water and Word, and says to us that we are special! Amid the problems, pains, hurts, and hopelessness of life, Baptism reminds us each day that we are affirmed.

**P** stands for *PROMISE*. Baptism is God's promise that He will never leave us. Even when we try to leave Him, even when we forget who we are, Baptism brings us back to the promise of God. And that's forever!

**T** stands for *TIME*. Baptism allows us to see that time is a gift from the Lord. God-given time can be used in special ways. As sponsors we can spend time with godchildren through prayer and through engaging in various activities with them. Time is a gift to be used wisely. As someone once said, "God invented time so everything wouldn't happen all at once!" Time allows us to see our Baptism happening in our lives each day.

**I** stands for *INDIVIDUAL*. Baptism calls us by name—we are individuals. We are not just a social security number, a zip code, an area code, or an e-mail address. We are individuals, named and saved through the blood of Christ. And because of that, we are people of promise. We are people who share this promise with others. There is only one of each of us—God loves us as individuals in Christ Jesus.

**S** stands for *STORIES*. We continue to tell stories about our faith life. We tell stories with our godchildren, with our sponsors, with those around us. "Those who tell the stories, define the culture." Wise words. People of God, people of Baptism, need to continue to tell the stories of love and joy and forgiveness in Christ. Tell the stories through Scripture, through personal experiences, through your church life, through your family. Continue to tell the story! We love to tell the story!

**M** stands for *MODEL*. Baptism makes us models of what it is to be baptized and forgiven people of God. We continue to model a life of forgiveness to those around us. We do not model perfection, but we model forgiveness. Forgiveness is not something we do. It is, first and foremost, something we are in Christ Jesus. It is a relationship we model through other people. We model ministry. We rub shoulders with others. We put people in caring, loving contact with each other. Our model is Christ, and Baptism allows us to be Christ-like to others!

Use each letter in the word Baptism to think through other faith experiences you have had. Baptism is not just a word, it is an experience of faith in Jesus Christ. Celebrate this faith today!

# Living Out Our Baptism

Our daily life is really just a living out of that baptismal promise. When I forget who I am in Christ and when I fail to live out the promise that God has given to me and all of my family members, the Spirit of God is present in the Gospel to remind me. The Spirit continues to connect me with God's baptismal promise that He will always love and forgive me.

Baptism is lived out each day in our daily relationships. The question is not "Were we baptized?" as if Baptism is simply an historical event. Instead, the question is "How are we living out our Baptism daily with those around us?" Martin Luther really did have a good idea when he suggested that we remember our Baptism each morning when we awake as we cross ourselves and get ready for a new day of promise.

Take time to look at your life to see the signs and symbols of your Baptism. In a sense, living out a life in God's baptismal promise is a way of reminding ourselves that each day is truly "a word from our Sponsor"!

In my office is a unique picture titled, "Christ." It is the kind that you need to stare at before you can see various images popping out from the myriad of colors. This picture is a great symbol of Baptism for me. Even when I cannot see the crucified Christ zooming out at me from the wall, I still know that He is in the picture. Likewise, even when I fail to remember my Baptism each day, even when I treat my own family members as if they are not baptized, and even though I forget my baptismal promise, Christ never forgets His promise to me and those around me. Baptism continues to be a daily activity as we remind each other that, *yes*, we truly are a family, one brought together through our Baptisms by God's love and forgiveness in Jesus Christ.

## So What Does This Mean?

How can we evangelically live out our daily life of Baptism? Here are a few suggestions.

1. Write down the Baptism date of each member of your family, including your godchildren. Post the list on the refrigerator door or some other significant place as a reminder. On each baptismal birthday, light a candle, bake a baptismal cake, sing a song, and do something special to celebrate the special day.

2. Keep close to the Word "from our Sponsor." In other words, connect yourself and your godchild to regular devotions, Scripture reading, and corporate worship with a community of faith. Remember, none of us is an island—we are all connected by the waters of our Baptism!

3. As a baptismal sponsor, help your godchild celebrate his or her baptismal birthday. Write a letter, make a phone call, send a special gift, affirm that person in the promise of Baptism.

4. Encourage your congregation to celebrate each Baptism in special ways. Perhaps families could make a banner, bring a candle, write a song, or send a card of celebration to those who are newly baptized.

5. Remind your family members and godchildren of Baptism through daily signs and symbols around them. A morning shower, a rainstorm, seashells, a cool breeze, a rainbow, a kind word and act—these are all gifts from God that connect the spirit of life with the promise of Baptism. As a favorite banner proclaims: "He is—and He is here—the signs are all around us!"

6. Remember your own baptismal sponsor. Why not write a note or call your sponsor? If your baptismal sponsor is no longer living, remember with joy the faith and significance of that person in your life.

7. Within your own family and with your godchildren, talk about what you remember about the baptismal service. Ask family members for their recollections about that special day. Who cried? Who laughed? What special prayers were offered or songs sung? Get everyone involved in remembering.

8. Do a word study about your godchild's name and your own. Ask your godchild what he likes about his name. What does she dislike? Share your own dislikes about your own name. Find out why the name was chosen. If you could have chosen your own name, what name would you have chosen? What is the root word of your name?

9. Talk daily about your Baptism. Put a sign on the bathroom mirror with the reminder *I am baptized!* Make baptism a household word.

10. Encourage your congregation to develop special prayers, liturgies, events, and opportunities for people to celebrate their Baptisms. As many congregations pray for each other on individual birthdays, they might also pray for each other on their baptismal birthdays.

God has called each of us by name—we are His! And that "word from our Sponsor" is really what keeps us together as we live, love, forgive, and care for each other, especially in the midst of the pains, problems, and messes in which we find ourselves. As baptismal sponsors, we are credible models living out the power and love of Christ in our lives for the children around us. As we live out the baptismal promise through examples of doing and telling; through our steady, patient, and positive witness; and through our life of prayer, worship, and service, we continue to shape children's images of God more than anything else around them. What a great God to mark us as our Sponsor! What a great God to forgive us and to promise that He will always call us by name. What a great God!

# Who Is Your Sponsor?

God is the "Sponsor" for all of His children. He sponsors us by continuing to forgive, love, and accept us. He created us, redeemed us in Jesus Christ, and continues to make us holy through the power of His Spirit.

Who was your sponsor at your Baptism? Who answered the questions, proclaimed their faith along with the entire congregation, and stated their commitment to pray for you and be intentional about bringing you up in the faith of our Lord Jesus Christ?

Thank the Lord for your sponsors today. If they are still living, contact them by phone, letter, or e-mail to say thanks for their support. Even if you have not been in touch with them for years, make it a point to connect with them. What a great way to thank the Lord and to live out your baptismal promise. If they have already died, pray for their friends and families who still remember them with hope and joy.

## *Your Baptismal Day*

How well do you remember your Baptism? Try to recall what you remember or at least what you remember your family telling you about it, if you were an infant. Was it a happy day? What special gifts did you receive? Did you cry?

Recall again words like the following that were no doubt shared with your sponsors and the worshiping community.

> From ancient times the Church has observed the custom of appointing sponsors for baptismal candidates and catechumens. In the Evangelical Lutheran Church sponsors are to confess the faith expressed in the Apostles' Creed and taught in the Small Catechism. They are, whenever possible, to witness the Baptism of those they sponsor. They are to pray for them, support them in their ongoing instruction and nurture in the Christian faith, and encourage them toward the faithful reception of the Lord's Supper. They are at all times to be examples to them of the holy life of faith in Christ and love for the neighbor.

> Is it your intention to serve as sponsors in the Christian faith? *Yes, with the help of God.*

> God enable you both to will and to do this faithful and loving work and with His grace fulfill what we are unable to do. *Amen.*

This was their promise to the Lord and to you. Even when our human promises fail and are forgotten, we are brought back to the promise of the Lord as the Spirit brings forgiveness, comfort, peace, and hope to us each and every day.

Before we move on to sharing more thoughts and ideas regarding your role as a sponsor, consider these special things that you can do for your baptismal sponsor.

1. Pray daily for your baptismal sponsors.
2. Write or call them regularly.
3. Be sure to remember them on their birthdays, both their natural and baptismal birthdays.
4. Visit them if possible. Spend time with them to recall the "good old days."
5. Make a videotape of yourself and the important people in your life today. Share it with your sponsors.
6. Think of other ways to affirm them, support them, and thank them for their support through the years.

# So You Are a Godparent

The parents of the newly baptized think so much of you that they have asked you to become a very significant person in their child's life. What an honor! This is much more than just showing up at the baptismal service. It is a lifelong commitment to be a "significant other" in the life of the baptized.

Someone once said that every baptized child needs to have an adult who is "crazy about them" as a friend and support person. That's not a bad definition of a sponsor! God puts us into relationships with people so we can share the joy and hope of the Lord in what we do and say with them. Deuteronomy 11:18–19 says it well:

> You shall therefore lay up these words of Mine in your heart and in your soul, and you shall bind them as a sign on your hand, and they shall be as frontlets between your eyes. You shall teach them to your children, talking of them when you are sitting in your house, and when you are walking by the way, and when you lie down, and when you rise.

These are great words for sponsors to remember as we continue to share our faith through the eventful and uneventful times of our lives. We continue to "talk and walk" our life of faith in the Lord!

Many years ago Mary Rita Schilke Sill wrote the poem "When You Thought I Wasn't Looking" for her mother, Blanche Schilke, to express thoughts about the power of our actions.

> When you thought I wasn't looking
> > You hung my first painting on the refrigerator
> > And I wanted to paint another.
>
> When you thought I wasn't looking
> > You fed a stray cat
> > And I thought it was good to be kind
> > to animals.
>
> When you thought I wasn't looking
> > You baked a birthday cake just for me
> > And I knew that little things were special
> > things.
>
> When you thought I wasn't looking
> > You said a prayer
> > And I believed there was a God I could always
> > talk to.

When you thought I wasn't looking
    You kissed me good-night
    And I felt loved.

When you thought I wasn't looking
    I saw tears come from your eyes
    And I learned that sometimes things hurt—
    But that it's alright to cry.

When you thought I wasn't looking
    You smiled
    And it made me want to look that pretty too.

When you thought I wasn't looking
    You cared
    And I wanted to be everything I could be.

When you thought I wasn't looking
    I looked . . .
    And wanted to say thanks
    For all the things you did
    When you thought I wasn't looking.

As sponsors we make a commitment to continue to share words and actions that reflect the promise of God that began in all of us at our Baptisms. That's the good news of our faith!


## So Who Should Be a Godparent?

Parents take very seriously, and appropriately so, the selection of godparents for their newborn child. Parents want someone who will continue to be a strong Christian model, supporter, and proclaimer of the love, joy, and forgiveness in Jesus Christ.

Significant thought was given to choosing you as a godparent. You were chosen as someone who shares your faith in the Triune God and believes as God's Word teaches about the nature and purpose of Baptism. An active Christian faith is a prerequisite for sponsorship.

In preparation for your role as godparent, consider the following:

1. How can I touch lives in positive and significant ways through faith-sharing and faith-living?
2. How do I demonstrate a strong Christian faith?
3. How can I exhibit a positive and celebrative style of life in Christ?
4. How can I be an effective model for my godchild now and as she grows older?
5. How will I remember to pray for, talk to, provide for, and even support my godchild through the coming years?

## The Responsibilities of Godparents

The main responsibility of a godparent is to model the life of a forgiven person of God in Christ Jesus to those you encounter in your daily life. Your role is to touch the lives of people—and especially your godchild's life.

You are asked to share your faith in the Triune God and to promise to bring up your godchild in the Christian faith. There are no legal implications for godparents. You are not being asked to be a legal guardian but rather to be an encourager, supporter, cheerleader, coach, mentor, tutor, and friend to the newly baptized. Your responsibility also includes a willingness to offer to your godchild encouragement and, when necessary, admonition. In addition, it includes support and affirmation of the parents, not as a "quasi-parent," but as a friend and affirmer.

Ideally, it is most helpful if sponsors can be in close proximity to their godchildren. However, because of the numerous transitions in life, often this is not the case. That means that godparents who are many miles away need to make a special effort to keep in touch with their godchild.

# Bible Verses for Baptism

One way that sponsors can assist parents is to help them select a special Bible verse for the Baptism. Study the Scriptures personally and select some verses that hold special meaning for you. Ask other family members to suggest some also. You can be helpful to the parents as you offer these suggestions. Here are some Bible verses to start your search.

I have called you by name. *Isaiah 43:1*

I will bring . . . health and healing, and I will heal them and reveal to them abundance of prosperity and security. *Jeremiah 33:6*

Let the children come to Me; do not hinder them, for to such belongs the kingdom of God. *Mark 10:14*

And He took them in His arms and blessed them, laying His hands on them. *Mark 10:16*

Ask, and you will receive, that your joy may be full. *John 16:24*

May the God of hope fill you with all joy and peace in believing, so that by the power of the Holy Spirit you may abound in hope. *Romans 15:13*

I give thanks to my God always for you because of the grace of God that was given you in Christ Jesus. *1 Corinthians 1:4*

Whatever you do, in word or deed, do everything in the name of the Lord Jesus, giving thanks to God the Father through Him. *Colossians 3:17*

But as for you, continue in what you have learned and have firmly believed. *2 Timothy 3:14*

Through Him [you] are believers in God, who raised Him from the dead and gave Him glory, so that your faith and hope are in God. *1 Peter 1:21*

But you are a chosen race, a royal priesthood, a holy nation, a people for His own possession, that you may proclaim the excellencies of Him who called you out of darkness into His marvelous light. *1 Peter 2:9*

See what kind of love the Father has given to us, that we should be called children of God. *1 John 3:1*

The following verses are Scripture references that can be used as baptismal stories to share in personal devotions and family celebrations or as special baptismal verses.

| | |
|---|---|
| Mark 10:13–16 | Acts 16:11–34 |
| John 15:1–17 | Acts 18:5–11 |
| Romans 8:1 | Acts 19:1–7 |
| Romans 16:9 | 1 Corinthians 12 |
| Acts 2:37–41 | 2 Corinthians 5:17 |
| Acts 8:9–25 | Galatians 3:23–29 |
| Acts 9:13–19 | Ephesians 2:13 |
| Acts 10:44–48 | Colossians 1:2 |

One of these verses could be the focal point in a banner you make to give to your godchild on this special day!

# Life Stages—
# Activities for Sponsors

The following is a list of activities that can be done in various life stages with and for your godchild. This list can also help you to develop other activities that can involve you and that special person.

## *Infants*
### *(birth to 2)*

- Pray for your godchild always!

- Buy a significant Baptism gift such as a cross, cup, or candle to be used on the anniversary of the Baptism.

- Take photos and videos of the Baptism. Send them to the parents with a nice note to your godchild. Be sure to add the date and your good wishes.

- Write a poem or song for her.

- Visit him frequently, if possible.

- Call the parents of your godchild throughout the year, expressing interest in her progress.

- Spend time teaching him Bible songs, prayers, poems, and fingerplays.

- Take her on outings—for ice cream, shopping, parks, walks. Spend regular "one on one" time with your godchild.

- Send cards and notes for special occasions—both to your godchild and to the parents.
- Send photos and videos of yourself so he can come to recognize you as someone significant in his life. This is especially important if distance separates you and your godchild.

# *Preschoolers*

### (ages 3 to 5)

- Pray for your godchild always!
- Continue many of the activities begun earlier, taking advantage of her growing language abilities. Develop a positive relationship bolstered by regular communication.
- Call on the phone and speak directly to your godchild.
- Take him on various outings—to the library, visiting with him at church and Sunday school, or going together to the ice-cream shop.
- Present a "You Are Special" plate or mug to your godchild to be used on baptismal birthdays.
- Offer to keep her overnight or for the day. What a great opportunity to develop a close relationship and have fun together!
- Send religious videos, books, or CDs for the child to use and enjoy.
- Encourage your godchild's parents to send him to a Christian school.

# School Age

- Pray for your godchild always!

- Send a children's Bible to her, perhaps on the baptismal birthday.

- Ask about school activities when you call and visit with your godchild.

- Share your own hobbies, talents, and interests with him. Explore similar interests together.

- Help to develop interests and talents such as singing, art, sports, collecting things, and other hobbies. Connect these interests with your faith and service to the Lord and His Church.

- Talk about your relationships with the Lord and the community around you. Be intentional about sharing forgiveness, love, and strong positive values in the Lord.

- Videotape yourself and your family on a regular basis and share these tapes with your godchild.

- Talk regularly about current events and what is happening in your life as well as in the world. Help her better understand your faith, your life, your joys, your values.

- Encourage, encourage, encourage!

# Confirmation Age
*(11 to 13 years old)*

- Pray for your godchild always!

- Be there on his confirmation day, if possible.

- Assist her in choosing an appropriate confirmation verse.

- Encourage him to look forward to new ways to serve the Lord as he begins high school.

- Encourage Bible study, youth group involvement, and regular worship attendance.

- Go on a bike hike, nature walk, train or plane ride. Take advantage of these times to talk about your feelings and faith together.

- See a movie or go out regularly for a meal—just the two of you. Discuss the movie and other issues in light of your faith and values.

- Get to know some of your godchild's friends. Help to be a positive influence in how her friends are selected.

- Attend school events—show your support and interest in what he is doing at school, church, and home. Be there for him!

- Encourage, encourage, encourage!

# High School Age
### (14 to 17 years old)

- Pray for your godchild always!

- Encourage your godchild to light her baptismal candle on especially good days—and also on especially bad days. It's a great reminder that we are always God's forgiven people.

- Do a servant event or a human care project in your community together. This is a great way to help others and share your faith together.

- Continue remembering him on special days. Send tickets to a baseball game. Attend events together. Or just call for no special reason.

- Continue to develop a close relationship with her so you can talk about anything—by letter, phone, or in person. Continue to be an adult model of forgiveness and trust.

- Discuss choice of dates, peer relationships, and other related topics.

- Discuss vocational choices together. What are his interests? Help your godchild make positive choices.

- Point out her strong points and affirm her special gifts.

- Encourage, encourage, encourage!

## Young Adulthood
### (18 to 21 years old)

- Pray for your godchild always!

- Give encouragement and support him in his choice of college or career. Visit possible schools with him.

- Pray together and discuss her goals—both long-term and short-term.

- Encourage your godchild to consider a career as a church professional.

- Send care packages or survival kits during final exam weeks or on his baptismal birthday.

- Continue to link your godchild with her parents. Be

a support and friend to all of them.

- Encourage, encourage, encourage!

## *Adulthood*

### *(22 years and older)*

- Pray for your godchild always!
- Affirm him in his chosen life's work.
- Be there for special days such as weddings, birth of children, and other transitions.
- Keep abreast of her church involvement and be supportive in every possible way.
- Invite him to your church or help him locate a church to attend.
- Invite her to visit you. Send a plane ticket as a birthday or baptismal birthday gift.
- Do things together that interest both of you—sports, travel, volunteer work.
- Encourage involvement in congregational life— through groups, study groups, various gatherings, and events.
- Continue to share your joys, your hurts, your concerns, and your faith together.
- Encourage, encourage, encourage!

# Celebrating Baptism through the Church Year

Here is a list of possible activities based on the liturgical calendar of the Church Year. Celebrate Baptism throughout the Church Year in these and other ways. Some activities can be done on your own to remind you of the significance of your role as a godparent. Others can be done with your godchild to strengthen your bond. What a great way to remember that Baptism is a daily experience.

## *Advent*

As we prepare for the coming of the Christ Child at Christmas, we can also prepare our lives and minds within a baptismal mind-set. Try these ideas on for size.

- Advent is a time for preparation. Think about how your Baptism is like the Advent season. List your thoughts and ideas.
- As you light each candle of the Advent wreath, remember your Baptism. Put a white baptismal candle in the middle of the Advent wreath and light it each day during Advent devotions.
- Make a family Advent/Baptism banner to hang in your home during the Advent season. Make one for your godchild to hang in his home.
- Call your baptismal sponsor and your godchild, asking how they are using the Advent season to prepare for Christmas.
- Notice the Advent/Christmas decorations around the house, church, and community. Discuss how these special decorations remind you of your Baptism.

## Christmas

- Send a Christmas card to your godchild and to your

own sponsors.

- Buy a Christmas gift for your godchild. It need not be costly, just a nice gesture.

- Think of children in your family, congregation, or community who would welcome a special card, greeting, or gift from you just because you want them to remember that they are loved by God.

- Do something special with your godchild during the Christmas season.

- Go caroling with family and friends to your god-child's home. Or go caroling with your godchild to some other home where the sounds of Christmas would be welcome.

# *Epiphany*

- Light your baptismal candle every day during Epiph-any to remind you that you are a light to the world because Christ is the Light to the world!

- Celebrate the Baptism of our Lord during the Epiph-any season in some special way. Ask your pastor to help you think of unique and creative ways to do this.

- Do a word study in the Bible on the word *light*. Let this study remind you that your Baptism has called you to be a light to the world.

- Write an Epiphany prayer and send it to your god-child.

- Have an Epiphany party for your family and friends. Invite your godchild also.

# Lent

- As you worship on Ash Wednesday, remember how God has marked you with the sign of the cross each day of your life.

- Decide to read at least one of the gospels during the season of Lent.

- Instead of giving up something for Lent, why not take up something for Lent? Perhaps you could take up a Bible study, attend a special Bible class, seek out the lonely and hurting each week, and help people see the Lord in their daily lives. If possible, arrange to do this activity with your godchild.

- Lent reminds us that we are sinners and have no hope without Christ. Look for examples in the daily news or on TV of the hopelessness around you. Pray to the Lord that people living without hope will learn of Jesus as the only Hope for the world.

- During Lent, spend fifteen to thirty minutes each day in silent meditation, reminding yourself that you are baptized. You may also want to use the ancient Christian tradition of making the sign of the cross on your forehead to remind you that you are marked by Baptism as a person of God.

# Easter

- Say and shout "He is risen! He is risen indeed!" to everyone you meet during the Easter season.

- Make an Easter banner to hang outside of your home to proclaim the victory of Easter.

- Color Easter eggs and give them to your godchild.

You might also throw in a few colorful candies.

- Send special Easter cards and maybe even a gift to your godchild.

- Make a poster to hang on the refrigerator door for people to write on. Start with the open-ended sentence, "Easter is like Baptism because . . . "

- If your congregation baptizes anyone on Easter Saturday or during the Easter season, send a special card or note to the parents and sponsors of those being baptized.

# *Pentecost*

- Sing "Happy Birthday" to yourself, to your family, to your godchild, to your friends. Pentecost is the birthday of the Church and you are the Church!

- Read the Pentecost account in the second chapter of Acts. Share it with a friend.

- Call or write to your godchild and wish her a "happy birthday." If she says, "It's not my birthday," remind her that Pentecost really is her birthday because she is part of the Church.

- If your congregation confirms young people during Pentecost, get a list of the confirmands and pray for them, send them a letter of congratulations, call them, encourage them to contact their baptismal sponsors, or think of other ways to help them celebrate their confirmation.

Today, think of ways that the Holy Spirit has worked through you to share joy and forgiveness with someone else. Not a bad thought for each day of Pentecost and throughout the Church Year!

# Baptism Celebrations

## Your Baptismal Birthday

More and more people are celebrating their own Baptism by lighting their baptismal candle and doing other special things on the anniversary of their Baptism. If you know that date, make a note of it and celebrate it. If you are unable to remember the exact date of your Baptism, it is appropriate to choose one so you might celebrate each year.

It is a Christian custom to celebrate the Presentation of our Lord forty days after Christmas. With this as a model, you could choose the date that is forty days after your birthday and "mark it" as your baptismal date.

## Baptism Celebrations in the Home

A gathering of people is a great way to celebrate the Baptism of your godchild or to celebrate the anniversary of a Baptism. Gather those who are special to the celebrant around the table or in the living room. Use the following forms as a means for sharing the joy of the baptismal day or use them on the anniversary of a Baptism.

You may want to have available photos of the baptismal day, the baptismal certificate, any gifts that were given, and other remembrances.

### Celebration Form I

1. Have the person being honored light the baptismal candle.

2. Begin with the Invocation: "In the name of the Father and of the Son and of the Holy Spirit. Amen."

3. **Leader 1:** *(Name)*, on this day in *(year)*, you were washed in the water of Baptism. Because of this event, you have been marked for life as a special person of the Lord. We rejoice with you this day as members of the family of God.

   **Leader 2:** Let us pray. God of love and forgiveness, we thank You for the promise You have made to *(name)* on this special day. Renew in *(name)* the gift of the Holy Spirit as he/she continues to trust in You and celebrates life each day. In Jesus' name we pray. Amen.

4. A meal or a snack may be served. Conversations could center around special stories from the Baptism, current stories of Baptism, and other significant family events.

5. Closing prayer. A designated leader leads the celebrating group in prayer, followed by the Lord's Prayer.

6. Final benediction: "May the God of hope fill you with all joy and peace in believing, so that by the power of the Holy Spirit you may abound in hope" (Romans 15:13).

## Celebration Form II

1. Begin with the Invocation: "In the name of the Father and of the Son and of the Holy Spirit. Amen."

2. In addition to the baptismal candle, use a special plate for the honoree. This plate could be used by each celebrant on their baptismal birthday. Place a bowl of water on the table to be used in this celebration.

3. **Leader:** "Arise, shine, for your light has come, and the glory of the LORD has risen upon you" (Isaiah 60:1).

4. Eat a meal together. During the meal, stories may be shared about the baptismal day and each day in the Lord. A special "toast" for the honoree may be given by someone significant in the life of the honoree.

5. After the meal, the leader says: "*(Name),* on this day in *(year),* you were baptized in the name of the Triune God. You were buried with Christ and raised with Christ. The Spirit came upon you and you were declared to be a child of God. You entered the family of faith. We give thanks for you and for the promises of God through Christ in Baptism. You are a forgiven, loved, cared for, precious person of God. And for this we rejoice!" (*Hoorays* and *alleluias* could be shared at this time!)

6. A brief Bible reading may follow. Suggestions include John 3:4–8, Acts 16:25–34, and Romans 6:1–4.

7. Join in prayer.

8. Share a sign of blessing with the honoree. Place a hand on the honoree's head and give a blessing. You might say: "May the promise of Baptism be yours each day, and may the Spirit continue to be your source of hope, comfort, peace, and love. Amen." Invite others to do the same.

9. Each person may take a turn dipping a finger into the water and making the sign of the cross on the honoree's forehead, saying, "You have been washed in Christ. You are a child of God. Hooray!"

10. Share the peace of the Lord, hugs, and handshakes.

11. The baptismal candle is extinguished. Final prayers and a benediction are shared.

12. The celebration continues as each person moves out into life, continuing to celebrate the promise of God in Baptism.

Additional suggestions for your celebrations include:

1.  Invite special friends to join in the celebration.

2.  If sponsors or other friends are unable to attend, videotape the celebration and share a copy.

3.  Share special gifts with the honoree. Think of small tokens that could be used as gifts to help people remember their Baptism (shells, photos, rainbow, cross).

4.  Sing hymns and Christian songs as part of the service.

5.  Invite the pastor and other professional church workers to join in the celebration.

6.  Discuss symbols and events in your lives that remind you of Baptism—a rain shower, a watercooler, shells, a rainbow, a new suit or dress, a glass of water, a hug, and other things around us.

# The Congregation as the "Shalom Zone" for the Baptized

Your congregation, the body of Christ, is the place where support and affirmation continues for the baptized child of God. It is not only the responsibility of the parents and sponsors to bring up a child "in the discipline and instruction of the Lord," it is also the role of the entire congregation!

That is why during the Rite of Holy Baptism the entire congregation is often asked to say a resounding "yes" to the fact that they, too, will pray for and encourage the spiritual upbringing of this child. Often a representative of the congregation professes, "In Holy Baptism God the Father has made you a member of His Son, our Lord Jesus Christ, and an heir with us of all the treasures of heaven in the one holy Christian and apostolic Church. We receive you in Jesus' name as our brother/sister in Christ, that together we might hear His Word, receive His gifts, and proclaim the praises of Him who called us out of darkness into His marvelous light." The congregation then responds, "Amen. We welcome you in the name of the Lord."

In a sense, what a sponsor promises to do for a godchild is the same as what the worshiping community promises to do for all of the baptized members in the congregation. What a responsibility! But what a promise and what a Lord!

The following activities can be done in celebration with and for your godchild, as well as for others in your congregation. Perhaps your congregation could begin to remember each person's Baptism this year by listing the names in your church bulletin and providing baptismal candles for each person. Your congregation could also consider making baptismal robes or banners and encouraging families to celebrate in special ways around their own family tables. Here are some other suggestions to enhance the baptismal celebration.

1. Develop a "Reaffirmation of Your Baptism" service as part of the worship schedule each year.

2. Encourage your pastor to emphasize the promise of Baptism in our daily lives often in his sermons.

3. Make a baptismal banner for each individual being baptized.

4. Hold classes about Baptism on a regular basis for parents-to-be and young families.

5. Consider putting visual reminders of your Baptism throughout the church building—banners, baptismal font, shells, and other reminders that Baptism is a daily event.

6. Give special baptismal gifts to all newly baptized individuals.

7. Write or call parents of newborn babies in your community. Offer your congratulations, send them a note about Baptism, and invite them to worship with you.

8. Make sure the children of the congregation can see and, if possible, be near the font during each Baptism.

9. Encourage young families with children, even infants, to worship regularly in your congregation. Invite them to sit in the front rows for worship.

10. Send out baptismal cards to each person in your congregation on the anniversary of their Baptism.

11. Give each first- or second-grade child in your congregation a Bible to remind them of the promise of Baptism. Present these Bibles at a special "Remember Your Baptism" worship service.

12. Each year, on the Sunday of the Baptism of our Lord, celebrate the Baptisms from the past year.

13. Hold a brainstorming session with your church staff, Sunday school teachers, or church council to consider additional ways to celebrate God's gift of Baptism for each person in your congregation.

# Prayers for Baptism

Lord, no person is an island; we are all brought together by water—the water of our Baptism. Help me to rejoice each time I see a Baptism happening. Help me to realize that I am also a part of each Baptism—You are giving me more brothers and sisters each time the water splashes and the Words of the Spirit are proclaimed.

Lord, it's fun to watch a Baptism happen. The parents are concerned that their little one is going to scream. I like it when they scream, Lord. I would too, if I were getting the devil knocked out of me! The sponsors are worried that they won't say the right words or that they won't be loud enough. The head usher is trying desperately to recall if he really did put water in the font. And the pastor is struggling to recall what the baby's middle name is!

Baptism is a great happening in our lives, Lord. Help me to remember who I am each day by remembering my Baptism. And help me to share the joy of this new birth with others in your family. In Baptism things happen. Thanks, Lord, for calling me by my first name! Amen.

(Adapted from *Pray, Praise, and Hooray,* © 1972 Concordia Publishing House.)

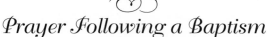

## Prayer Following a Baptism

Lord, it was a great baptismal service. It was great to hear the resounding yes from the congregation as they promised to take care of our godchild. It was great to hear the parents and us saying yes as we promised to love and care for this child.

Help us to take this service and relive it each day of

our lives. Help us to see that Baptism is not a "one shot deal" but a daily experience of faith. Help us to continue to say yes to You, to our Baptism, and to this new child of Yours.

Thanks, Lord, for this baptismal service. And thanks for Your resounding yes to us as Your people! And we say it again, Lord, in Your name. Yes, yes, yes! Amen. Thank You for the promise to me and to my godchild. In Jesus' name. Amen.

## Prayers for Godchildren

Lord, I still remember seeing my godchild for the first time. What a beauty! Maybe all infants are beautiful, but this one was special! My godchild is special because You have called and loved this person in a special way. Help me now to do all that I can to continue to love my godchild also.

I do worry about my godchild, Lord, with all the hurts, hopelessness, pain, and messes in the world. I get afraid. In my times of fear, send Your special measure of comfort and hope to me. And help me be a source of hope to my godchild in every way possible.

We are going to make it, Lord, because You have promised. Keep this promise before us. In Your name. Amen.

○

Lord, what a gift it is to be a godparent. To think that You think enough of me to trust me with one of Your precious creatures. I'm awed and amazed!

Help me, Lord, to not only show my good side, but more important, to model that I am forgiven through my Baptism for all the bad I do.

Help me to walk and talk the faith that You have given to each of us. And when my godchild goes astray and forgets about You, and even me, draw this person back to You in every way possible. And if You need to use me, I'm here, ready for the call!

Forgive us, Lord, when we forget about You. Move us, Lord, to help each other see Your presence in our lives. Help us to celebrate Your power and presence among us. In Jesus' name. Amen.

◯

Lord, thanks for bringing my godchild into my life. Help me to know how to express my concern, to listen with understanding, and to share the joys of living. Help my godchild to see me as a model of You realizing that I am not perfect, but that I have perfection in Your sight through the blood of Christ and because of my own Baptism.

And help my godchild to see me as a person who needs love, affirmation, and encouragement. Sometimes I don't feel so good about myself. Please help my godchild to love me in spite of my faults and mistakes.

Help me to remember the various ways to show my love to my godchild. Through the years help me to keep in touch, keep my godchild on my prayer list, and above all, to reassure my godchild of my love and appreciation.

Thanks for calling us as Your children. In Your name. Amen.

◯

Lord, I've gotten out of touch with my godchildren. I'm not even sure where they are anymore. Wherever they may be, please watch over them, protect them, and continue to give them Your promise of love and hope through their Baptism.

Help me to remember them through my prayers and, if I ever do connect with them again, help me to share Your love for them. Thanks for making Your love so evident in my life. Now help me make Your love for them evident in their lives also. In Your name. Amen.

# Prayers for Parents

Lord, it is sometimes hard to figure You out. How You bring people together in families is beyond me. I wonder what You had in mind by bringing the parents of my godchild and my godchild together in the first place. There is much stress, turmoil, and pain. You know it better than I do, Lord. Use me as an instrument of healing. Use me to be a bridge of love and forgiveness between my godchild and the parents.

When I said yes to being a godparent, Lord, I knew I was saying yes to a significant role. I did not take godparenting lightly. And I still don't. But give me the strength to be one source of comfort, hope, and peace as they struggle daily in their relationships. Help me, O Lord. You promised. In Jesus' name. Amen.

Lord, I don't know how parents do it. Schedules, ball games, mealtimes, homework, workloads, pressures, travel, finances, clothes, parties, on and on and on. It never quits!

Especially today I pray for the parents of our godchild. Give them the strength, the power, the humor, the encouragement, the forgiveness that only you can give. When they are ready to call it quits, to cave in, to say "It's not worth it," give them that extra nudge of love and peace.

Lord, You continue to move us, strengthen us, and put people in our lives who support and encourage us so we can somehow get through. Do the same for the parents of our godchild. Please, Lord. They need it now. In Your name. Amen.

# Call Me Lucky

The story is often told of a lost-and-found item in the newspaper that reads:

> Lost Dog: three legs; blind in left eye; missing right ear; tail broken; recently hit by a truck; answers to the name Lucky.

Have you ever felt that way? I have! Yet isn't it super that our Lord still calls us lucky? Because of our Baptism and His love and forgiveness through the death and resurrection of Christ, we are the lucky ones as God continues to pour His blessings upon us.

And now it is our task to go out and tell others how lucky they are to have a Lord who refreshes, renews, and forgives.

Just call me lucky!

## Reflections

1. When do you most often feel lucky? Why?

2. Who needs some words of forgiveness and comfort right now, maybe even from you?

# A Baptismal Journal

Use the following page to display a Baptism picture of your godchild, noting the child's age and the date of Baptism. Thank the Lord for health and growth—spiritually and physically—as you look at this photo.

Use the journal pages to record thoughts, feelings, and observations. You may want to write a special letter to your godchild so he can later recall and remember these special experiences.

The journal pages could also be used to record conversations with your godchild, activities you've done together, questions you may want to ask your godchild, and other significant observations and details. Use these pages to reflect, to pray, and to remain close to your godchild.

# Baptism

PLACE PHOTO HERE

# Baptism

*Reflections on this special day*

_____
_____

*Memories to keep*

_____
_____

*My prayer on this day*

_____
_____

*Bible verses to remember*

_____
_____

# My Growing Godchild

*Reflections as my godchild grows*

_____
_____

*Memories to keep*

_____
_____

*My prayer on this day*

_____
_____

*Bible verses to remember*

_____

_____

# Confirmation

*Reflections on this special day*

_____

_____

*Memories to keep*

_____

_____

*My prayer on this day*

_____

_____

*Bible verses to remember*

_____

_____

# High School Graduation

*Reflections on this special day*

_____

_____

*Memories to keep*

_____

_____

*My prayer on this day*

_____

_____

*Bible verses to remember*

_____

_____

# Other Significant Events

*My reflections*

_____

_____

*Memories to keep*

_____

_____

*My prayer for my godchild*

_____

_____

*Bible verses to remember*

_____

_____

# A Closing Word from Our Sponsor

Baptism—not something we do for God, but something God does for us. Claiming us as adopted children is God's gift to us. What we do with our lives is our gift to God.

Sponsors, godchildren, and parents are all part of the body of Christ in partnership through the power of His Spirit.

> For just as the body is one and has many members, and all the members of the body, though many, are one body, so it is with Christ. For in one Spirit we were all baptized into one body.
> *1 Corinthians 12:12–13*

What a great word from our Sponsor—each day—as we live out the promise of Christ in the family of God.

## *I Am Baptized*

Martin Luther was baptized on St. Martin's Day, November 11, 1483, at the Church of St. Peter and Paul in Eisleben, Germany. Throughout his life he celebrated and affirmed this baptismal event. Whenever he was in doubt or in despair, tormented by the devil, he would cry out "I am baptized!"